Spin Your Own Wool
and dye it and weave it

MOLLY DUNCAN and her husband, the late Mr J. E. Duncan, compiled the New Zealand Department of Agriculture's bulletin *Spin Your Own Wool* which was first published in 1943 and ran for edition after edition before finally going out of print.

Mrs Duncan has had many years of experience in spinning and also in dyeing, using both chemical dyes and vegetable dyes made from Australian, New Zealand and exotic plants. She has studied home weaving at the Sturt Craft Centre, Mittagong, New South Wales, and at the Sydney Annual Loom School. She has travelled widely in both the United States and Britain lecturing on weaving, and studying weaving practices in both countries. A second book, *Creative Crafts with Wool and Flax* was first published in 1971.

SPIN YOUR OWN WOOL

and dye it and weave it

by MOLLY DUNCAN

Line drawings by Erica Duncan
Photography by George Bull

REVISED AND ENLARGED EDITION

a Bell Handbook

G. BELL AND SONS LTD,
LONDON

First New Zealand Edition 1968
published by A.H. & A.W. Reed Ltd

First British Edition 1973
published by G. Bell and Sons Ltd,
York House, Portugal Street,
London, W.C.2.

ISBN 0 7135 1740 9

I0527534

Typesetting by New Zealand Typesetters Ltd, Wellington
Printed by Dai Nippon Printing Co. (International) Ltd, Hong Kong

Contents

List of Illustrations

List of Figures

Introduction

SPINNING, DYEING, AND WEAVING are the three parts of one whole craft, so that when you venture into any one of these activities your interest is kindled in the other two, and a practical understanding of all three will develop. Sooner or later what began as a hobby will develop and expand into a craft.

But is this craft worth pursuing when machines can produce the finished product so much faster and more efficiently? From a severely practical angle the answer is, decidedly, "No". But if you think of spinning, dyeing, and weaving as an interesting, useful, and creative occupation the answer is, even more decidedly, "Yes".

Whether this occupation is an art or a craft, the textile craftsman is needed to supply that extra dimension that comes only from handwork—the making of threads, their colouring, their blending, and their weaving into a harmonious result. All this requires skill and a sense of design. The fascination and challenge for the craftsman lie in his or her opportunity to create the unusual—something that simply could not be mass-produced by machines.

This book was written primarily as a comprehensive guide to the processes involved in making threads, specifically the spinning, scouring and dyeing of wool. However, it also provides a short introduction to the more intricate processes of weaving which have been more fully explained in a second book entitled *Creative Crafts with Wool and Flax*.

Acknowledgments

I am indebted to my late husband, J. E. Duncan, for the technical information contained in his Department of Agriculture Bulletin *Spin Your Own Wool*. In this book I have endeavoured to expand and continue his work.

I wish to thank my daughter Erica Duncan for the production of the line drawings and George Bull for the photographs, without which this booklet could not fulfil its purpose.

I acknowledge the kind permission of the Director General of Agriculture for allowing me to revise my husband's bulletin; and I thank the staff of the New Zealand Wool Board Technical Services Laboratory for much help and advice.

M.D.

1

Selecting Your Wool

FIRST AND FOREMOST a knowledge of one's raw materials is necessary to achieve harmony between the fibres selected and the final woven pattern. Australia and New Zealand both offer the most versatile natural fibres for experimentation and discovery: wool in both countries of exceptional high quality, and the easiest of all fibres to spin and dye; cotton in Australia that can be hand-spun for slub or novelty effects; and New Zealand flax, that weaves so well in textured wall-hangings and introduces that earthy natural appearance sometimes necessary in a tapestry.

Of all the natural fibres used for spinning, wool is the easiest material for both Australians and New Zealanders to obtain in suitable condition for spinning. For this reason wool-spinning forms the main subject of this book, but the same techniques can be applied to the spinning of both cotton and flax.

No longer is the spinningwheel a romantic relic of the past or a decorative piece of old furniture – it is much in demand and decidedly functional. More and more farmers are interested in the possibilities of using their own wool, either as hand-knitted or handwoven garments for wearing apparel or as warm blankets for the household. Both wool stores and skin and hide dealers are making wool available for the private buyer.

And no longer is the black sheep an outcast of the flock, such is the demand for its varying shades of greys and browns and the natural wool blends made from them.

A spinner will need to be selective of her wools depending on what she wishes to make. Although it is possible to spin any type of wool grown in Australia and New Zealand the beginner would be well advised to avoid the extremes; that is,

the very long and the very short fibres, the very coarse and the very fine.

For preference select a fine crossbred having a * count of 48/50s and a staple length of 4 to 6 in. Also a suitable fleece should be reasonably even throughout and open in character (avoid cotted or matted wool), should be of good colour (not stained by weather or artificial colouring matter), and contain a reasonable amount of yolk or "condition", i.e., natural grease. It is important to make sure that the wool is sound and does not have a bad "break" or weak spot. A single staple or lock when held by the ends should withstand a fairly vigorous pull without breaking.

The old saying is true that "it takes fine wools to make fine fabrics". The Merinos that flourish so well in Australia and produce the finest wools grown in New Zealand will spin into a very soft yarn suitable for babies' garments and for adults' lightweight cardigans. But these fleeces are often extremely short in staple length and so very fine that they are difficult for a beginner to spin. Acquire a reasonable degree of skill first on the Corriedale and Merino halfbred wools which are fine, but not as fine as Merino. These wools lie in the count range of 56s to 58s and are longer in the staple and more easily spun than Merino.

In the crossbred wools such as Romney, Romney-Cheviot, Leicester, and Border Leicester wools which are all available in Australia and New Zealand the count range is from 46s to 50s, and these wools are even longer in the staple than the halfbreds and are very easily spun.

All the wools just mentioned will spin a knitting yarn. When asking for wool from a wool merchant try to describe what you require in terms

*A count is the the measurement of the fibres diameter

of count range, as this will make it easier for him to select your needs. Ask for Corriedale or half-bred 56/58s if you want fine wool, and for cross-bred wool 46/50s or 48/50s if you require something coarser. State that you want it well grown, sound, showing good character, and colour, then you will get a good spinning wool.

Coarse crossbred with a count lower than 46 and hairy wools and most second-shear (which are short-fibred) wools will be more difficult to deal with. They need to be spun into a thicker yarn and woven into floor rugs, or blended in small quantities with finer wools to make textured and/or fleck effects. These coarser and shorter wools are often the prize selection for the crafts-man wishing to create a yarn or fabric of a dis-tinctive character most suitable for woven sculpture. (No wool, not even skirtings, need be wasted.)

It is possible to get very pleasing effects by the use of naturally coloured wool such as black, brown, or grey either by themselves or in con-junction with white wool to give a 2-ply marl effect. Try equal weights of white and coloured and/or two parts of white to one part coloured. For even colouration these must be teased and carded into rolags ready for spinning. These make attractive shades of fawn and light grey. For lighter tonings still, ply these with a single-ply white.

2

Spinning

SPINNING "IN THE GREASE" is the term used when wool is spun directly from the fleece with no preparation. No extra oil is added and no teasing or carding is required. Any top-quality fleece newly shorn and with a good staple length is better spun "in the grease". Just hold the wool in the left hand and with the right hand draw out the fibres from the bottom end of the staple nearest the shearer's cut, feeding them slightly sideways into the twisting yarn and keeping them parallel. In some old fleece the natural grease or "yolk", as it is called, becomes dry and hardened. The addition of olive oil or a mixture of neatsfoot oil and washing soda will help the staples to open out and thus facilitate spinning. Olive oil is the more expensive product but the neatsfoot and soda are easily mixed and keep well. Dissolve 4 oz. of washing soda in ½ gallon of water and add this to the oil until a milky emulsion is formed.

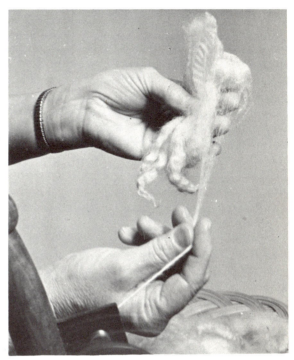

Spinning in the grease.

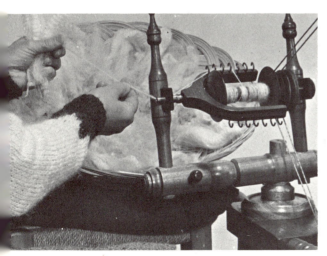

Spinning in the grease.

Keep a saucer of this mixture handy while you are spinning, and frequently dip your fingers in it. Alternatively, keep the mixture in any plastic squeeze-bottle and shake it over the fleece wool. It is wise to leave the fleece wool with the added oil lying for a day or so before carding or spinning, as this gives the oil time to become evenly distributed throughout the wool. Mineral oils such as those used for lubricating motorcars and machinery must be avoided, as they will not wash out during the later stages.

If your fleece wool has already been scoured, i.e., washed free of natural grease, it can still be spun even though it is dry and harsh to feel. Apply a liberal amount of olive oil to the wool itself and to your fingers when spinning.

Often parts of a fleece will require *teasing;* and wool that is to be carded and blended should be teased first. This is quite a simple job and entails the opening out of the individual staples or locks with the fingers into a fluffy mass. It will be found easier and quicker to pull the staples apart sideways rather than endways. Hold the bulk of the wool in the left hand and pull away small pieces at a time with the right hand. While you are doing this it is easy to remove any pieces of vegetable matter such as thistles, burrs, etc., and also any very short or matted pieces of wool which would be difficult to card. These short bits of wool should not be thrown away because, although unsuitable for spinning, they will be found useful after being washed for filling cushions, or weaving into finger-twisted bags and rugs, to mention only two uses.

All spinners search for the top-grade fleece of even crimp and regular staple length that can be spun direct from the fleece, but not all wool is so obliging. Even the best of fleeces will have some parts that are short in length and need the time-consuming process of carding. This may be done with just a steel hair comb, a metal dog-comb, or a discarded blade from a shearing machine. Only the tips of the wool staple need to be combed to open out the uneven, matted, discoloured ends. Hold the staple tightly in the left hand and comb the tips, keeping the wool fibres as much as possible in their staple form. To avoid scraping your fingers with the comb place a piece of hardboard on your lap or on the edge of the table. Hold the wool tightly over the hardboard and comb on it.

Carding with carders is a more difficult process but one that all spinners and weavers need to learn. Carders are two flat pieces of wood with handles, the wood being covered on one side with leather into which are inserted bent wires or hooks, all bending towards the handles. It is advisable always to use a left-handed carder in the left hand and a right-handed carder in the right hand. In this way there is less wear and tear on the hooks and the carders become compatible. Mark the carders distinctly, left and right.

Take the left-hand carder in the left hand with the wires uppermost and the handle pointing to the left. Place a small portion of fleece wool lengthwise on the wires of this carder, that is, the fibres of the wool staple running parallel with the side edges of the carder and not across.

Right: With right-hand carder comb the wool several times.

Below: Wool placed lengthwise on the left-hand carder.

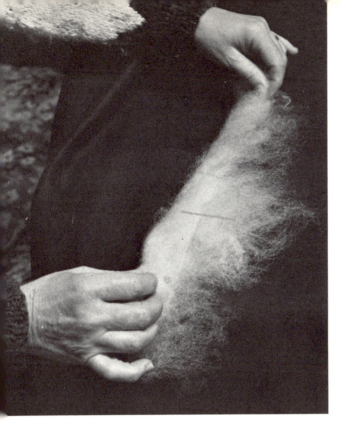

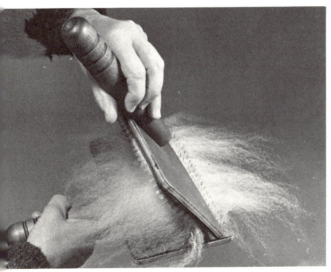

Above: Stripping wool off the carders.
Top left: Rolling a rolag.
Bottom left: Transferring the wool from one carder to the other.

With the second carder in the right hand stroke the wool down several times as if combing it. Thus a straight fringe of fibres will protrude from the edge of each carder and some of the wool from the left carder will become entangled on the teeth of the right carder. Take care that the fringe is not doubled over, causing tangling. The principle of carding is to keep all fibres running lengthwise, the same as in a staple of wool. Remembering this principle, wool can be transferred from one carder to another for further treatment.

When the wool has been sufficiently carded it has to be stripped off both sides. Hold both carders upright and apply the outer edge of the right carder to the outer edge of the left. A downwards pull of the right carder will now strip most of the wool off the left. Now reverse the process by pulling the left carder downwards to strip the wool off the right. The wool should now be sufficiently loose to be free of the carders. How many times to repeat these actions will depend on the character of the fleece. Do not attempt to place too much wool on a carder at one time — overloading will cause folds and tangles.

After the soft loose mass of fibres has been shaken free from the two carders, the orthodox procedure is to let it fall on the back of the left carder and then roll it with the back of the right carder until it assumes the form of a loose cigar-shaped roll 7 to 10 in. long and 1 to $1\frac{1}{2}$ in. in diameter. This is called a "rolag" (fig. 1).

Some carders are not flat on the back owing to the projecting manner in which the handles are fitted, and do not lend themselves to the making of rolags. In this case it is easier to make the rolag by rolling the fluffy mass of wool on the table with the hands.

have already dealt with; next, the drawing, entangling, and twisting will demand a little practice.

The purpose of twisting fibres together is for strength, and their drawing out makes the continuous yarn. Smooth fibres such as flax, linen,

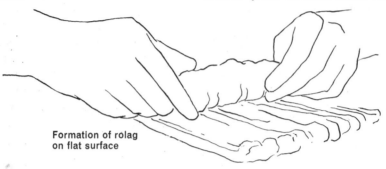

Formation of rolag on flat surface

Fig. 1. The fluffy mass of carded wool being rolled into a "rolag".

The test of a good rolag is to hold it up to the light; it should present a uniform open appearance throughout with no dense parts or patches of short, tangled, or knotted fibres. These all lead to difficulties in spinning and imperfections in the yarn; if they are numerous, it indicates that further carding is required. If there are only a few, they can easily be picked out and removed with the fingers. To make a continuous yarn with these rolags is the next consideration.

Test of a good rolag.

Spinning today is just what it was in the old days: a continuous process of arranging the fibres, drawing them out, entangling, and twisting them to produce a length of yarn. The first process we

cotton, and silk are more difficult to spin because the fibres slide past one another; but wool, being crimped in length and scaly and rough (look at it under a microscope) hooks and clings together when twisted. Furthermore, to aid the wool-spinner in her task, each wool fibre has a small oil gland which lubricates the fibre in its entire growth. Thus a freshly shorn fleece is always easier to spin because the oil is still soft, thus lubricating the twisting fibres while they are being spun.

Learning to spin can be accomplished on a very elementary piece of equipment called a spindle. In fact, until the early part of the sixteenth century the spindle was the only means available for producing a twisted yarn. Even today some Australian Aborigines spin rabbits' fur on a primitive sort of spindle – three sticks tied together, one long one with two shorter ones tied to function like the disc or whorl on our spindles.

A modern spindle consists of a thin round piece of hardwood dowelling about 12 in. long with a hook at the top (a long crochet hook is a good substitute) and a disc or whorl at the bottom. This disc gives the spindle momentum so that you can spin it like a top. The softness and lightness of spindle-spun yarn makes it particularly attractive for knitting. When plied into 2-ply or

3-ply yarn it is quite a strong thread, and one that is not easily over-twisted and tight.

How to spin with a spindle (fig. 2)

a. Take a piece of already-spun wool about a yard long and tie it to the spindle as at 1 in the illustration. Carry it round the pillar of the spindle below the whorl and over to 2. Catch the wool in the slot with a half-hitch. (To do this have the wool on the right-hand side of the spindle, place the forefinger of the right hand behind the thread, then twist the finger backwards over it, thus forming a loop which is slipped on to the hook.)

Fig. 2.   Learn to spin on a handmade spindle.

b. Take a rolag or teased piece of fleece and let it lie over the back of the left hand.

c. Pull out a few strands of the fleece – enough to twist it into a stout thread.

d. Fluff out the end of the spun wool and lay it with the strands of the rolag between the thumb and first finger of the left hand.

e. With the right hand twist the spindle like a top in a clockwise direction and you will feel the wool making a twist and becoming yarn.

f. Continue to pull out the strands of the rolag and twist the spindle until it drops to the ground.

g. To wind this spun yarn round the pillar of the spindle slip the yarn from the notch at top, remove the thread from under the whorl and then wind it criss-crosswise up and down the spindle shaft. When full it will be packed into a neat cone and will slip off the spindle shaft easily.

h. Yarn spun in the direction described above is known as Z-twisted, while yarn spun with an anti-clockwise spin of the spindle is an S-twisted yarn.

Hold the fleece wool fairly tightly between the thumb and finger of the left hand to prevent the twist going too far into the rolag. Join on another rolag when necessary, as at the beginning, by laying the fluffed ends together. When the spindle becomes too full and heavy and it seems as though its weight may cause the yarn to break, untie the beginning thread and slide the completed cone on to a stand.

Spinning on the spinningwheel

Progress demanded a much quicker method of making a continuous yarn than using a simple spindle. Both hands needed to be free to control the speed of the twisting thread, so the wheel with a driving-belt evolved – at first hand-operated, and later treadled with the foot.

The spindle, instead of hanging vertically, now lies horizontally between two uprights – the whorl revolves by means of a driving-belt or string that passes around the whorl and around the rim of a much bigger wheel. This is the simple basic principle of any spinningwheel.

Improvements evolved on both the spindle and the driving force – a tapered metal rod replaced the wooden shaft, leather bearings were adopted to hold the revolving shaft, a grooved whorl to take the driving-band, a tension device to vary the amount of twist.

Before applying the technique of making a continuous yarn learnt on the hand-spindle to making one on the spinningwheel, it is wise to get the feel of pedalling the wheel. Use the rhythm of *Row, row, row your boat, gently down the stream* to develop a steady regular pedalling, which must be practised until you become familiar with your wheel. Also try stopping the wheel when it has just passed its highest point so that when the action is resumed the wheel does not reverse its movement. Make sure that all moving parts of the wheel are well oiled and then you should be ready to start.

a. Place an empty bobbin on the spindle and tie tightly to this bobbin the end of an 18-in. (or more) length of spun wool, or soft string that does not slip.
b. Take this thread over the nearest hook on the flyer and thread it through the hollow end of the spindle. This is most easily done by pushing inside the hole in the spindle a hairpin or similar bent bit of wire or a crochet hook, until it can be seen from the "eye" or hole in the side. It is then easy to push the string through both eye and hairpin, and draw it

Joining rolag to the spun yarn.

out. Another useful thing for the same purpose is a short length of spring curtain rod; if the last three or four turns are stretched out, they form a miniature "corkscrew" which easily catches in the string or woollen yarn and pulls it out through the spindle.
c. Now see that the brakeband is properly in position in the groove in the bobbin, and that there is some tension on it.
d. Take a rolag in the left hand and wrap a few fibres from it round the spun yarn or string already on the spindle. This should be Z-twisted, since the metal rod of the spindle will

Drafting of the fleece wool.

be turning clockwise. Now start to treadle, slowly at first.
e. It will be found that the end of the string will start to revolve too and, if it has been laid correctly, it will immediately entangle and pick up some of the loose fibres of wool in the end of the rolag. If correct tension has been applied to the brakeband, there will also be a tendency for the string to be drawn in through the hollow spindle.
f. Now is the time to speed up the rate of treadling, drawing out the fibres and allowing twist to run up towards the left hand which holds the rolag. This principle of drawing out the yarn to even it and controlling the degree of twist and thickness is known as drafting. When spinning from

rolags and with practice, longer and longer drawing-out or drafting of the fleece wool becomes possible (fig. 3). It is this rhythmical control of the twisting yarn between both hands that makes the successful spinner. Which hand does the drafting and which one releases the twisting thread into the "eye" of the revolving spindle is immaterial – the spinner herself will choose the most comfortable position and will adapt her techniques to suit the position of the spindle on her particular wheel. Adaptations are almost automatic when once the principles of spinning are understood.

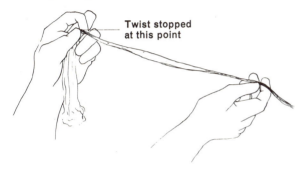

Twist stopped at this point

Fig. 3. Drafting. The thickness of the yarn and the amount of twist are controlled by the two hands.

g. Two things should now happen simultaneously. The spun thread should be drawn through the hole in the spindle and wound on to the bobbin; and the twist should run up the wisp of wool fibres towards the rolag. If too much twist runs into the rolag, stop spinning and dangle the rolag down below the spindle and it will unwind itself to a certain extent.

Strive to make an even thread, no matter how thick at first – try to avoid a thread that is very kinky and tightly twisted in the thin places and very weak and poorly twisted in the thick parts. Throughout the drafting process if that steady regular treadling is maintained a more evenly spun thread will be made. This is a good rule to remember: "Hands fast, feet slow to spin; hands slow, feet fast to ply."

If the yarn is not feeding on to the bobbin and becomes more and more twisted check the follow-

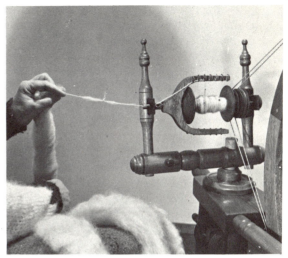

Strive to make an even thread.

ing: first your tension on the bobbin brakeband. If this is too loose an over-spun thread will result. Adjust this according to the type of tension control on your wheel. The whole function of a brakeband is to retard the speed of the bobbin slightly below that of the flyer. On the other hand, if the tension is too great the yarn is pulled away from the spinner's grasp and the thread is lost through the orifice before twisting has taken place.

Secondly, make sure that the wool has not caught around a hook; or that your spinning may be too thick to pass through the eye of the spindle. Both of these faults will stop the yarn winding on to the bobbin and increase the twist. As spinning proceeds remember to change the thread to the different hooks on the flyer so that the bobbin fills more or less evenly and thus spins evenly.

Plying wool

The thickness of the yarn spun can be varied a good deal according to the wishes of the spinner, but even if thick enough, the single-ply yarn is not always suitable for knitting. To make it stronger it is necessary to ply two or more strands together —most spinners ply two. To do this, place two full bobbins of single-ply yarn on the bobbin holder or "lazy Kate" as it is called (fig. 4). The ends of these yarns are tied to the "leader" (the short length of wool usually left on a bobbin to facilitate starting) so that they are twisted together and wound on to the bobbin as a 2-ply yarn.

Two points in the procedure differ, however, from ordinary spinning. Firstly, the tension on the brakeband is considerably increased, so that the 2-ply yarn will wind on to the bobbin without assistance, the two strands merely passing between the fingers as a guide. Secondly, the direction of rotation must be reversed. This is done simply by treadling the wheel in the opposite direction; where an electric sewing machine is used to drive the spindle and the motor cannot be reversed, the same effect can be obtained by crossing the belt.

For 3-ply place three bobbins on the lazy Kate and proceed as for 2-ply. To make a soft yet

singles, loose ply). Coloured ply yarns vary enormously – try plying two different coloured singles, or a hand-spun with a machine-spun thread, or introduce a synthetic yarn.

Skeining

The next stage is to place the full bobbin of 2-ply on the lazy Kate and wind it off on to the skeiner. Figure 5 shows how to wind on to the skeiner with an over- and under-motion so that while the skeiner itself is 18 in. long the skein when removed measures 36 in. when stretched over the fingers. Before it is removed from the skeiner, however, the skein of wool should be tied in four places with string to prevent it tangling when being washed.

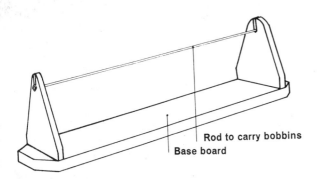

Fig. 4.   The bobbin holder or "lazy Kate".

strong knitting yarn, spin the singles finely and with just sufficient twist to hold them together, but ply these with as little spin as possible. Plying needs to be fairly firm for hard-wearing yarn, but remember it looks tighter on the bobbin than when skeined.

Plying offers many interesting variations with both colour and texture for both hand-knitting wool and for unusual handwoven materials. A Z-twisted single, plied with an S-twisted single, gives a texture different from that of two Z-twists together, or two S-twists, because the process of plying adds twist to one and reduces it in the other. Texture varies .also when singles are spun loosely but plied tightly – and vice versa (tight

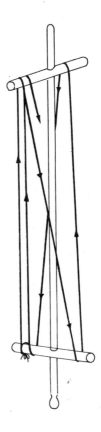

Fig. 5.   The skeiner. How to wind the yarn over and under.

3

Choosing Your Wheel

SOONER OR LATER the possession of one's own wheel becomes desirable – though it does not necessarily guarantee the ability to spin a good thread! Certainly a good well-balanced wheel makes the task of the spinner easier, but just as much patience and practice is called for on the good wheel as on the simple spindle. However, speed of production favours the spinning-wheel and even more speed if the wheel is motorised. Concurrently, the speed of the drafting must be quickened to prevent the spinning of too tight a yarn.

Let us then consider the pros and cons of certain spinningwheels or spinning attachments, remembering always that the buyer may be restricted to a price range which may restrict his or her choice. When buying a spinningwheel there are certain features that the buyer must consider, for there are now available quite a number of different styles of wheels and several attachments designed to be run from sewing machines, either treadle or electric. Also there are wheels so well finished that they have an additional value as graceful pieces of furniture. The price range, therefore, varies remarkably.

Our consideration will be with wheels for functional purposes. Spinningwheels can be either horizontal or upright. The less expensive model being upright but the horizontal setting has a more attractive appearance and it allows more space for a larger wheel and more space for the feet when treadling. On the other hand, the horizontal wheel occupies more floor room in an already over-crowded modern home, and is not easy to store in a cupboard.

Some models have sloping tables, others straight and set very low. This is a matter of appearance and does not affect the functioning of a well-balanced wheel. Originally the table was sloped to make room for a larger wheel. Now for the same reason the table is set low, but in addition, you can use the straight table to place some of your equipment on without it sliding off.

The height and position of the legs also vary. This is important to the stability of the wheel – splayed-out legs prevent the wheel toppling over. With short straight legs a wheel takes less space in a room and is easier to pack away or crate for transportation, whereas too-short legs will cramp the position of your feet when treadling.

Hard wood is usually chosen for the construction, not necessarily for appearance, but to add weight to the wheel so that it is less inclined to slide away from you as you are spinning. At this stage it may be good advice to emphasise – *never* buy a wheel you have not seen. It may not be "your" wheel. Comfort in spinning is one of the first considerations, as a spinner will be many hours at her wheel requiring a good relaxed position for easy rhythmical spinning.

The mechanical features to examine are listed below and the diagrams name the parts and their functions.

a. The wheel should be reasonably true and well-balanced, not warped, not buckled, and with no wobbles.
b. It should revolve smoothly and evenly, requiring very little effort to treadle. The larger the wheel, the slower the pedalling can be.
c. There should be some effective means of adjustment for the driving-belt to take up any slack which may develop.

d. The flyer and bobbin should be capable of revolving rapidly and smoothly without undue vibration and noise.

e. The best design is that where the spindle revolves in thick leather bearings, as these are silent, oil-absorbent, and long wearing. Furthermore, the flyer and bobbin should be between these bearings; those designs which have them over-hanging one bearing are very prone to vibration and noisy running.

f. All machines have some means of giving the bobbin and the flyer different speeds of rotation. In the older machines this was achieved by two driving-bands, one for the bobbin and one for the flyer, which were fitted with different-sized pulleys. This system gives no scope for the separate adjustment of the bobbin speed and is inferior to the type where the flyer only is driven and pulls the bobbin round with it, but at a slightly lower speed because of an adjustable brakeband which retards the bobbin. This brakeband usually consists simply of a string tensioned by means of a peg which is twisted. Make sure that whatever system is used it works properly, for on this adjustment successful spinning largely depends.

g. The bobbins, of which there should be at least four, should all be of the same size, and should run truly.

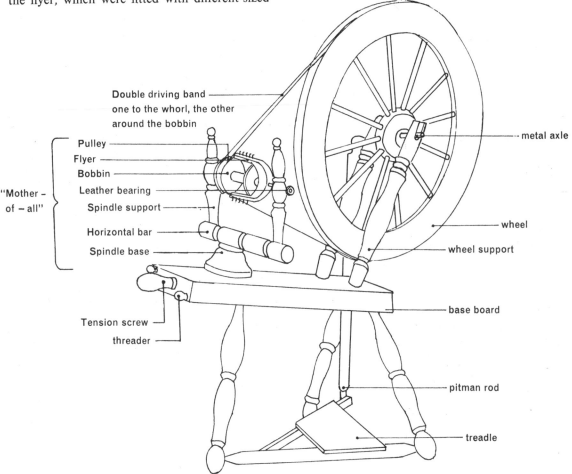

Fig. 6.   The wheel and its parts.

Here is a final good test for your wheel: slip off the driving-cord and, if the axle is well oiled, the wheel should continue to revolve 15–20 times after you stop pedalling.

The wheel and its parts

The unit including the spindle base, the spindle supports, the spindle with its flyer and bobbin, has a delightful oldfashioned name, "mother-of-all". For brevity and sheer pleasure I will use this term. See fig. 6. (Opposite page).

During the long history of spinning wheels many variations have evolved in the construction of the "mother-of-all", and a close look at the step-by-step developments and the reasons for each step may help in the understanding and the selection of your wheel. The simple hand spindle placed horizontally and held in bearings, was revolved by a band passing around the spindle and then around the drive wheel, both spindle and wheel moving in the same direction. The drive wheel was manipulated by hand and, of course, could be turned clockwise or anti-clockwise. The yarn was twisted, and the wheel then stopped while the spun thread was wound on. This stopping of the wheel slowed

down the production. To overcome this the flyer mechanism was developed.

Stage 2 The spinning wheel becomes more decorative. The spindle is supported between two uprights called "maidens". The whorl developed in different ways. The mother-of-all is moved as a unit backwards and forwards to tighten or loosen the driving belt.

Stage 1 in the development of the spinning wheel. The vertical spindle (see Fig. 2 Page 15) is now held horizontally. A driving band passes round the whorl and continues round a groove in the rim of the wheel. One hand is occupied turning the wheel, the other controls the spinning from a carded rolag.

As this is a walking wheel the height of the wheel had to suit the spinner.

A whorl showing several grooves. Notice that the spindle is tapered to a sharp point and may, or may not, have a slight groove like a very blunt crotchet hook.

The flyer is also known as the guider, as it holds the metal hooks that guide the spun yarn along the bobbin. It is U-shaped or horse-shoe-shaped and the hooks are arranged on both sides to maintain good balance as well as to distribute the yarn evenly along the bobbin. The yarn coming from one set of hooks will build up in ridges along the bobbin and when changed to the other side these ridges will be levelled out. [Figs. 7 & 7a]

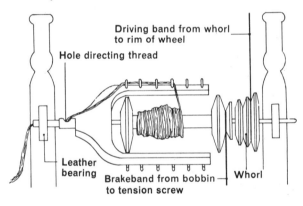

Fig. 7. Diagram of the complete "mother-of-all" that moves backwards and forwards to control the tension

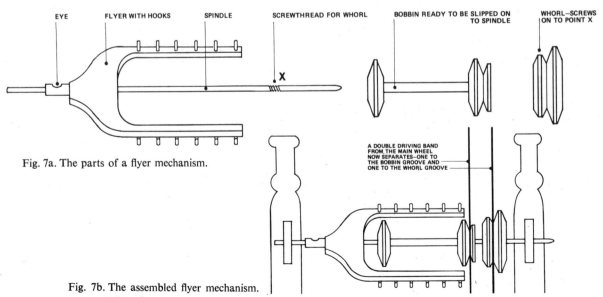

Fig. 7a. The parts of a flyer mechanism.

Fig. 7b. The assembled flyer mechanism.

The Spindle is also called the needle as it is made of metal and has an eye at one end through which passes the twisting yarn. The flyer is fixed to the spindle near the eye approximately $\frac{1}{2}$-1 in along the shaft. At the other end of the spindle a thread is cut in the metal on which the wooden whorl is screwed. The driving band from the big wheel fits into grooves in the whorl. Both flyer and spindle rotate together. Most spinning wheels have these two units attached firmly together and labelled as "the flyer"; others have them separated and when in use the flyer is wedged on to the spindle which is tapered at this point to receive the flyer. When buying a wheel of this kind make sure these two units wedge together tightly as they tend to come apart with the continuous rotation.

How tension is controlled by moving the complete mother-of-all backwards and forwards (fig. 7)

Set the tension screw that shifts the mother-of-all to about the halfway position. Wind string or tightly-twisted cord round the rim of the wheel, then round the spindle whorl (this has two grooves, ignore the front one at present). Pull the cord tight and sew the ends together very firmly. Adjust the tension screw until the cord is taut. Start the wheel by hand in a clockwise direction and treadle at a slow even pace. If the treadling seems laborious slacken the tension screw, thus bringing the mother-of-all nearer to the revolving wheel. Check that all moving parts are well oiled – the axle bearings, the leather bearings holding the spindle, the metal pins on the legs, and where the pedal and driving shaft meet. Remember to set the leather bearings, holding the metal spindle shaft, at right-angles to the shaft. If the pressure against the spindle is too great it becomes impossible to spin at all. When a bobbin is empty and first put in position it may be necessary to slacken the tension screw by a half-turn (or slightly less): a full bobbin tends to retard its own speed with the added weight. Referring back to the spindle whorl with its two grooves, the larger diameter one is known as the weft groove for softer spun thread, the smaller diameter (nearer the bobbin) is the warp groove for making a thread with a tighter and firmer twist.

A brake-band added for tension control

This is another type of tension control found on many wheels; where a corded brakeband passes round the bobbin groove to a special tension screw. This screw when adjusted advances or retards the speed of the bobbin and does not move the mother-of-all. If this brakeband were not there both the flyer and bobbin would revolve on the metal shaft at the same rate, and the spun yarn would not wind on at all. The amount of tension needed is surprisingly slight – if too taut neither bobbin nor flyer will move – then with a small adjustment of the peg the rates of both the winding-in of yarn and the degree of twisting can be balanced.

The position of the tension peg is important as the brake-cord must lie at right-angles to the spindle and bobbin.

— Driving band

Brakeband —

Fig. 8. Spinning wheel with whorl attached to the spindle in front of the flyer. A brakeband is added for tension control of the bottom. The driving band is tightened by raising the mother-of-all.

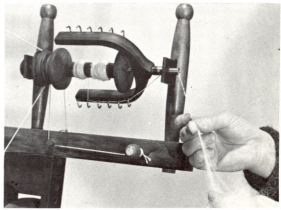

The peg near the top hand can be turned to adjust the brakeband tension.

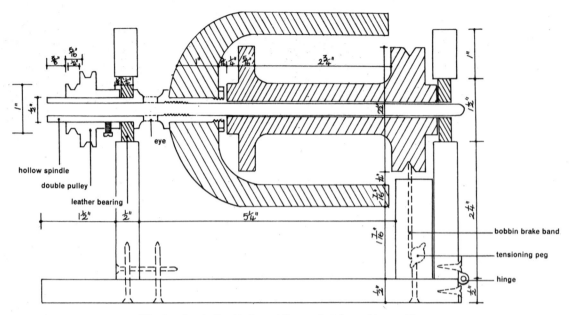

hollow spindle
double pulley
leather bearing
eye
bobbin brake band
tensioning peg
hinge

Fig. 9.   A spindle attachment for an electric sewing machine.

Detailed dimensions of a spindle attachment to run from an electric sewing-machine motor designed and made by J. E. Duncan (fig. 9)

The end support swings out on a hinge when the hook is lifted, making the bobbin easy to remove, and leather bearings are pivoted on steel pins to facilitate this. The bobbin brakeband terminates in a light coil spring, which gives smoother running and compensates for any inequalities in the bobbin.

Any electrically-driven spindle revolves faster than a pedalled one. To compensate for this it is necessary to draft and to feed in the yarn more quickly. Correspondingly, the amount of wool spun is greater. This attachment can be adjusted to meet the needs of some handicapped patients incapable of using any pedalling mechanism, and many spinners keep one of these attachments entirely for plying, in order to increase their output.

Shows left-end support hinged to remove bobbin.

Shows spring-tension control.

4

Scouring, Bleaching, Dyeing

IT IS DESIRABLE, sometimes, to clean the skeins of spun yarn from dirt and vegetable matter and yet retain the natural yolk or grease to make the knitted garment showerproof. Using enough cold water to completely cover the skeins steep them for several hours in this cold water to which has been added a small quantity of Lux liquid or similar detergent. Rinse thoroughly.

Scouring

This is the process of washing wool till it is completely free of natural grease and dirt. The best results are obtained by using warm water (120° F (50° C), i.e., as hot as the hand can bear) to which has been added detergent. The proportion recommended: 1 dessertspoon of detergent to 1 gallon of water, and ½ teaspoon of common salt.

Detergents are preferable to soap, for if the wool is to be dyed later any slight alkaline residue of soap left in the skeins will react on the dyes and spoil the finished product. Do not rub or agitate the skeins unduly but rather squeeze gently in the hands to avoid tangling and felting. If the wool is very dirty it may need a second wash with more detergent before it is finally rinsed in plenty of warm water. Do not wring the skeins but hang them in the sun and wind to dry. A weight tied to hang from the wet skein will stretch out any kinks in the spinning. Ammonia added to the scouring water will yellow any white wool to a certain degree.

Bleaching

At this stage the spun wool may be quite white enough and ready to use, particularly if it is a merino wool, but some varieties of fleeces show a creamy or yellowish tinge which, if not desired, must be bleached.

This is done by first dipping the skeins in a hot solution of Condy's Crystals (potassium permanganate). Proportions are ½ teaspoon of crystals to 1 gallon of hot water (150° F). Keep moving the skeins gently – in fact, it is a good idea to hook your skeins over a ruler or stick. Lower half the skein into the solution and, as it turns brown in the Condy's Crystals, shift the skein round the ruler until the other half is brown also.

Next, immerse the brown skeins in the bleaching solution. The chemical used is sodium dithionite (sodium hydrosulphite) which is the basis of many bleaching agents sold by the chemists. Proportions are: 3 teaspoons of sodium dithionite to 1 gallon of hot water (120°–150° F).

In a few minutes that brown skein will change miraculously to an off-white and the bleaching process is complete. Rinse the skeins thoroughly in warm water.

Always use warm–hot water (120° – 150° F) as wool wets twice as quickly in warm water as in cold. (This applies also to the dye bath as well as to bleaching, as the wool will absorb the dye more evenly in warm–hot water.)

Dyeing

It will not be long before a handweaver and spinner requires colour in the finished work, because it is through colour and design, the two being correlated, that the craftsman expresses himself when once he has mastered the techniques of the craft.

Tone values – the making of the fibres lighter or darker than the rest, the blending and carding of colours for fleck textures – can change the

Flax flower.

whole character of the finished work. To get these shadings the craftsman must dye his own colours.

Chemical dyes are just as essential as vegetable dyes, both having certain advantages and disadvantages. It is the tone values of both chemical and natural dyestuffs and their degree of fastness that are important to all spinners and weavers. Certainly, vegetable dyeing has a fascination all its own because of the beauty of its results, the aromatic smell, the soft mellow colourings that tone so well with the natural fleece wools and, above all, the joy experienced with surprise results. But too many soft tonings often make the finished article appear weak and insipid – to bring out brilliance and character a chemical dye is essential – one helps the other for the best results.

However, any yarn, no matter how beautiful in colouring, is valueless unless it stands up to the conditions for which it will be used. Test all your home dyeing for fastness to light by placing a part of your hank or skein in a closed box and allowing the other half to be uncovered and

exposed to strong sunlight. A vegetable-dyed yarn, if it fades, does so in a more pleasing toning than the fading of a chemical dye. The easiest colours to obtain in vegetable dyes are the off-white, fawns, yellows, browns, and brown-greens; we must rely on the chemical dyes for the best blues, bright greens, and red shades.

Wool, having fibres that are porous, is one of the easiest fibres to dye. It can be dyed either in the skein or loose before spinning, but the wool in either case must be washed clean and be free of grease.

How to use chemical dyes

The quickest, the easiest, but the least rewarding method is to purchase from any chemist a good reliable *boiling* dye of the colour of your choice (not a cold-water dye); follow the directions carefully and correctly, and dye your spun wool in the skein.

Immense pleasure and knowledge can be gained by selecting boiling dyes of the three basic colours (red, blue, and yellow) and mixing them to the shadings you desire. The colour possibilities derived from the basic reds, blues, and yellows are

Tamarillos (tree tomato).

Lichen.

shown on the "colour-wheel" on the back of this book.

Take three clean glass jam-jars, one for red, one for blue, and the third for the yellow. Into each jar place a portion of dye, sufficient to cover a one-cent piece. Take a pint of warm water and pour equal quantities into the three jars. Dissolve the dye thoroughly. A drop of liquid Lux to each jar will help to dissolve the dye. Into a measuring cylinder or its equivalent pour your own colouring mixture, e.g., 2 fluid oz. of blue, 2 fluid oz. of yellow, 1 fluid oz. of red. Hold the measuring cylinder up to the light to see if it is the colouration you wish. If not, alter the colouring accordingly, using the colour-wheel as your guide.

Partly fill any suitable rustproof vessel with lukewarm water, pour in the resultant dye mixture, add a little acetic acid (½ teaspoon of acetic acid to 1 gallon of warm water). Stir well, and lastly add the wool which has been wetted previously in lukewarm water. Very slowly bring to the boil at a steady rate (not less than 20 minutes) and simmer very, very slowly for not more than 20 minutes, turn off the heat and allow the wool to

remain cooling in the dye bath for another 20 minutes.

The wool must be completely covered by the dye all the time it is in the dye-bath otherwise uneven dyeing will result. Gently prod the wool with a wooden spoon or stick to keep it submerged but don't violently stir or agitate it too much or it will cause felting. Watch carefully during the simmering stage that the water does not boil away leaving some of the wool exposed – if this happens, add enough warm water to cover the wool again.

The value of the small quantity of acetic acid to the dye-bath is to swell the wool fibres and enable them to take up the dye more readily, thus adding fastness of colour.

By and large, ordinary tap-water is soft enough to be used for all scouring, bleaching, and dyeing in New Zealand. Australian home-dyers would be well-advised to use rain water, or to add a little vinegar to their tap-water to soften it, particularly if their water supply is artesian, which is usually very hard. (This also applies to limestone areas in New Zealand such as the Oamaru district, where the water is hard.)

Lichen.

Blue gum leaves.

Dyeing with vegetable dyes

As with chemical dyes, vegetable dyes can be used either when the wool is loose, before spinning, or the yarn may be dyed in the skein. Dyeing the loose wool means extra work, as the wool has first to be scoured before dyeing and then well-oiled again afterwards before it can be spun. For certain things this extra work is inevitable. Dyeing the loose wool will also give the most even shades where only one colour is used, for any irregularities of shade will be levelled out in the carding process, which thoroughly mixes and blends the wool.

The next question is, what vegetable materials to use? The field is wide open for experimentation – any plant that yields a colour when boiled, any bark of a tree when softened that releases a juice, berries, fungi, lichens, seaweeds, and even the good earth itself, particularly red volcanic mud and black soil from the swamps. Of all these, lichens offer the most interesting colourings. Whatever the plant used it is desirable to make notes about the source of material, the time of the year when

it was gathered, and the exact conditions under which it was used, so that you'll know how to reproduce the same shade at a later date.

Basically, there are two classes of natural dye-stuffs:

a. *Non-mordant* dyestuffs, sometimes referred to as substantive dyes because the colouring matter extracted in the boiling fixes itself permanently on to the wool fibres. Lichens belong to this class but they have the added distinction of developing different tonings if used with a mordant, particularly with acetic acid, or potassium bichromate, or both of these combined together. Dry-looking lichens need to be soaked for at least 24 hours in water just sufficient to cover them.

Then there are two ways of dealing with this softened lichen: either boil it to extract all the colouring matter first and later add the dampened wool and treat as described for chemical dyeing, i.e., slowly bring to boil not under 20 minutes, simmer very gently for 20

Red gum.

Wattle.

minutes, and cool in the dye-bath not less than 20 minutes. Or, place the wool in some butter-muslin bags and make alternate layers of wool with layers of lichen – simmer a little longer than the previous method, $\frac{1}{2}$–$\frac{3}{4}$ hour depending on the colour you require and the state of the wool. (Some wool will matt horribly if stewed for a long time.) The former method has a more gentle effect on most wools. Both methods respond equally well to tests on fading qualities. For strong colouration from a lichen that releases its colour well, allow 4 oz. of wool to 8 oz. of lichen.

The real challenge in dyeing with lichens is to find the ones that release the rich "orchil" colouring, which is the name given to the red juice (the colour of blackberry juice) extracted by fermenting a lichen with ammonia, water and oxygen. An orchil doesn't always remain red— it can change to a dark bluish shade when exposed to the air after a long period of fermentation. With every lichen you gather, particularly those that are bursting into new growth, make a test experiment for the orchil dye. Take a small glass jar with a tightly fitting lid. Into it place some of the lichen that you have dried, and

crumble it into a powder (this helps to get quick results). Pour into the jar a strong solution of half ammonia and half water, shake well, seal the jar, and leave for a day or two. The oxygen enters by stirring. At first stir 5-6 times per day (replacing the lid immediately) and reduce to 3 times a day as soon as the red colour begins to run. To aid fermentation place in a warm place. If your experiment yields the "orchil" dye and you wish to use a large quantity of lichen treat it in the same way except for the strength of the ammonia solution. Reduce it to one part of household ammonia to two parts of water. Also it may not be practical to powder a quantity of lichen. If it is dry roll it with a rolling pin between two sheets of newspaper as you would do dry breadcrumbs. If it is a green and moist lichen mince it in your kitchen mincer. Sealing your container, stirring, and macerating in a warm place are all equally important.

b. The second class of natural dyestuffs are those that require a *mordant*, which is a chemical substance that acts as a link, binding the dye to the wool fibre. Mordants most commonly used in the vegetable dyeing of wool and the ones most readily procurable are alum, bichromate of potash, iron sulphate (also called copperas or green vitriol), stannous chloride (tin crystals), and cream of tartar.

There are two ways of dealing with these mordants and you will need to experiment to gain the colouration you require.

First, the wool can be mordanted before dyeing – then re-dampened and dyed in several different dye-baths for a variety of shades.

Or, the mordant, the dye, and the wool can be boiled together in the same dye-bath. This is by far the quickest and easiest method.

The following proportions for each mordant listed here may be a guide for your experiments:

Alum (potassium aluminium sulphate). 3–4 oz. of alum to 1 lb of dry, clean, scoured wool. The smaller quantity for fine wool or light shades. Dissolve the alum thoroughly before putting in the damp wool. Use the same method of bringing slowly to the boil, simmer gently 20 minutes and cool slowly.

Cream of tartar (potassium bitartrate). This is not a satisfactory mordant used by itself but is used as a modifying agent with other mordants for different shades. With the above alum recipe use: 1 oz. cream of tartar, 3–4 oz. alum, 1 lb of wool.

With tin crystals use: ½ oz. tin crystals (stannous chloride), 2 oz. cream of tartar, 1 lb of wool.

Bichromate of potash (chrome). ¼–½ oz. of chrome, 1 lb of wool. Use as described for the alum method. Chrome tends to deepen the colour on lichens and is worth trying with other plants together with acetic acid.

Onion.

Iron sulphate (copperas, green vitriol). ¼ oz. of iron sulphate, 1 oz. cream of tartar, 1 lb of wool. These colours are dark. It is wise to keep a vessel exclusively for this dye since it is difficult to scour away all traces of the iron except from a stainless steel vessel.

Tin crystals (stannous chloride). ½ oz. tin crystals, 1 oz. cream of tartar, 1 lb of wool.

Acetic acid. 40 per cent solution as procurable from the chemist, ½ teaspoon to 1 gallon of warm water. In all vegetable dyeing, as with chemical dyeing, and for the same reason, a little acetic acid should be added to the dye-bath, or to the wool before entering it into the dye-bath.

Fastness of colour

Quite naturally home-dyers are concerned always about the fastness of their colours. Certain vegetable dyes recently tested on a laboratory "dye-fading" machine have proved surprisingly good.

Bright yellow shades were the first colours to show a change.

A dusting of yellow spores on paper-like lichens usually give stronger colours.

Bark, berries, lichens, and plants were used in the tests, with colours ranging from light fawns to rich cinnamon-browns, bright yellows to maize shades, mauve-brown to purpley-browns, and soft greens. Because the sources of dyestuffs vary enormously in different districts and are subject to seasonal changes as well as to the varying methods of treatment in the dye-bath, this investigation was not an exhaustive study but a revealing one within its limitations. For example, pigeon berries (porokaiwhiri) mordanted with alum and cream of tartar gave a soft canary-yellow which faded within one day in bright sunlight; but the same berries mordanted with potassium bichromate gave a ginger-gold shade which stood the test in the fading-machine as well as any of the other dyes. On the other hand, puriri berries mordanted with alum and cream of tartar gave a rich purpley-brown and was a fast colour. The seed-pods of New Zealand flax in four varying shades of tans depending on the strength of the dye-bath, gave excellent results for fastness. So, also, did the bark of towai (*Weinmannia*) of the North Auckland species, which yielded a pinky-fawn with alum but a soft grey with iron sulphate. All the colour range from lichens that were tested proved satisfactory except for the bright yellows. A delightful green extracted from parsley from the home-vegetable garden mordanted with copper sulphate ranked also as a fast colour.

For all of us who indulge in the delights of vegetable dyeing the homely method of testing our work by exposing to strong sunlight (see page 25) is very reliable indeed.

5

An Introduction to Handweaving

A HANDSPINNER doesn't necessarily have to become a handweaver, but a handweaver is nearly always a spinner as well because her work calls for attractive threads which often must be handspun. Nevertheless, the interest in weaving is present in most of us, and more and more spinners are anxious to try it.

For this reason I am including this section on handweaving mainly to increase spinners' understanding of the different yarns which feature so prominently in the textile craft of today. Twines, twists, and textures become an obsession with the enthusiast to such an extent she examines even machine-spun fabrics with new eyes, and analyses it for its threading, its pattern, and its colour combinations.

I have used the title of this section – an "introduction" – advisedly, as handweaving deserves a book to itself. Furthermore, more advanced weaving requires larger looms with more shafts and pedals for the wider range of pattern work. Correspondingly, the larger the loom, the greater the financial outlay. True – it is good advice if you are purchasing a loom to acquire an all-purpose large 4-shaft with 6, 8, or 10 pedals and one that will take a 48-in. material, but not every modern home would have the space to house it.

Still, there is much creative work that can be accomplished on smaller, less expensive, looms involving "tabby" weave only. For this reason I have confined this section to writing about plain weaving and what can be accomplished on hand-made inkle looms, 2-shaft table-looms and rug-making looms, all of which are easy to thread-up and which all offer wide scope for design, colour, and texture.

Any weaver on a multiple-shaft loom will acknowledge the fact that after tying up the 6, 8, or 10 pedals it will be the two that are tied for tabby that are used the most. Pattern work followed from a book becomes repetitive – it's some one else's design – and somehow the joy of invention and ingenuity is lost. Plain weaving, well executed and with a correct balance of threads, has charm in its very simplicity. Most pattern weaves need the contrasting plain to high-light the pattern for good design. Nor does plain weaving need to look like the machine-made product if the weaver selects his raw materials and yarns with imagination.

Plain weaving is often referred to as tabby weaving but there is a distinction between the two in the texture, though not in the threading and the pedalling. A tabby-woven piece of material should show 50 per cent of warp and 50 per cent weft, whereas plain weaving does not necessarily do this. Both are like darning – a simple "over one and under one" interlacing of threads. The warp is the measured lengths of threads that are attached from end to end of any loom. The weft is the thread used to fill in – to interlace like darning across the width of the loom.

Let us consider the potential of 2-shaft weaving under the headings of colour, irregular denting, and yarn combinations. Inlays, tufting, pick-up leno, and brocades can be postponed until pattern work is studied.

Colour offers the widest range of variations in weaving. Be bold with it. Use bright colours in the warp whenever possible, remembering that when woven they will lose some of their strength and give different tones and half-tones. If a striped warp is used and a plain weft, the stripes on the material will be vertical. If a plain-coloured warp is used with different coloured weft stripes, the stripes in this fabric will be horizontal – these will become more interesting if a thicker weft yarn is used such as gimps, slubs, and other fancy twists. Evenly spaced stripes in both warp and weft produce checks. A light warp background can be woven with a dark thread for the tabby weft to give a deeper tone to the original warp threads, and vice versa – a dark warp will become lighter by using a light shade for the weft.

To help in the selection of colours try winding them around a ruler or notched stick in either broad or narrow bands until you achieve a pleasing sequence. With a blunt wool needle, darn a few rows across to get a better idea of the tone effects.

Also try to make certain warp colours predominate by using a pick-up stick. This can be done by raising one shaft and picking up every second thread on this shed, thus passing over three and under one thread. Or, leave the shed down and pick up every two threads along the weaving.

Irregular denting. Meshes or open weaves are made by missing dents across the reed and weaving with weft spaces to match. It is a safe rule to weave a small sample first, then wash and iron it to see if the chosen yarns are suitable. Smooth plied yarns are not suitable in tabby meshes as the groupings slip and disappear after laundering. Homespun wool lends itself very well to this form of texture work.

Yarn combinations. Here I would recommend the handweaver to start a collection of fabric samples 6–8 in. square because it is only by seeing and feeling different woven yarns that experimentation begins to yield its rewards. So many yarn-combinations are available for this – thick and thin yarns, lustrous and dull, fancy and plain, varying twists, hand-spun and machine-spun. All have to be wisely chosen, remembering always that the resultant fabric must wear well and be suitable for the purpose for which it is intended.

There are a few do's and don'ts worth recording. When combining coarse and fine yarns in the same material, which undoubtedly adds effect and

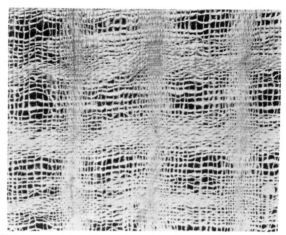

Pattern resulting from irregular denting of single-ply homespun wool.

character, watch particularly for any distortion of the fabric – to prevent this, increase the number of fine threads in relation to the number of coarse ones. A harmonious balance of threads is necessary to avoid puckering. Measure your sample square exactly.

A finished fabric is nearly always more pleasing if a correct balance of the same kind of yarn is selected for both warp and weft, e.g., a woollen material looks and feels right if wool is used for the warp also, rather than a cotton warp with a wool weft.

LOOMS

The easiest loom of all to make and operate are inkle looms. The small model can be held on your knee and operated while you watch television. A larger model can be made to stand on the floor and be high enough for the weaver to sit at comfortably on a low chair.

How to make an inkle loom (fig. 10)

Materials required:
    5-ply wood, 24 in. by 12 in.;
    2 pieces of scrap wood for the stand;
    6 old camera spools or dowelling;
    cotton to make heddles – Anchor Pearl No. 8
      or 2/12 cotton yarn;
    5 screws and washers, one wing-nut.

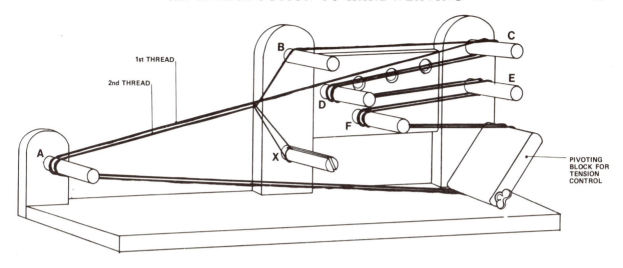

NOTE PEG X IS SPLIT TO HOLD THE HEDDLES SECURE

Fig. 10 a   An American type inkle loom

Cut the 5-ply to the exact dimensions given on the plan. Smooth the edges with a wood rasp to prevent threads catching on any rough edges. Cut a slot for peg D, as this peg must be adjustable so as to tighten the warp ready for weaving. For a standing floor model make the slot at peg D run vertically, by so doing a longer length of weaving can be accommodated. Screw the camera spools to the inkle loom at positions A, B, C, E, and X, as shown in diagram. Peg D, attach with washer and wing-nut. Nail or screw to stand. Height recommended for the floor model is 2 ft 6 in. from peg B to the floor.

To make the string heddles

Cut four dozen pieces of cotton 10–12 in. long. To find the correct size to knot these heddles, stretch a string very taut between pegs A and C. Loop a heddle string over this and knot it below peg X. The function of peg X is to hold these heddles. Knot with a reef-knot the four dozen pieces of cotton exactly the same size and slip them onto peg X.

To mount the warp

Begin the winding of the warp at peg A. Temporarily fix the beginning of the warp thread on camera spool A with sticky tape. Take your thread across the loom from left to right, passing between the pegs B and X, then round C, D, and E and back to A. This forms a continuous circle.

On the second round take the thread through the first of the cotton heddles, up and over the top of peg B and then around the rest of the pegs, C, D, E, and back to A.

Take the third thread straight across (not through a heddle) between pegs B and X, as in the first round.

The fourth thread goes through the next cotton heddle and over peg B like the second.

Carry on thus until the warp is completed, i.e., the number of threads you calculate for the width. Note that all the warp threads that pass through a heddle must go over the top of peg B, the alternate threads go straight across passing under peg B.

To weave in the weft

This consists of lifting and lowering the warp threads to form a shed through which the weft passes. On the lower threads between pegs B and X press *down* with your hand. This makes the first shed. Insert your weft thread across. Place your hand *under* the lower and raise them up above the level of the cotton heddle loops to form the second shed. Pass your weft thread back.

Inkle looms can make strips from 42 in. long (as described in the small model here) to a floor model making 6–7 ft depending on how large the frame is made and the extension of the outer adjustable pegs. The position of peg X is not altered as it holds the cotton heddles. If wider strips are required use wider pegs and not camera spools which can only take up to 2 in. in width.

Now beat the weft threads back towards peg A with a ruler or any flat thin stick on which you have wound the weft yarn. Change to the first shed and continue weaving in the same way.

As the strip grows it will be necessary to shift the warp round the loom back towards peg A. This is done by loosening the bottom peg D and retightening afterwards.

Pressing lower threads down with your hand.

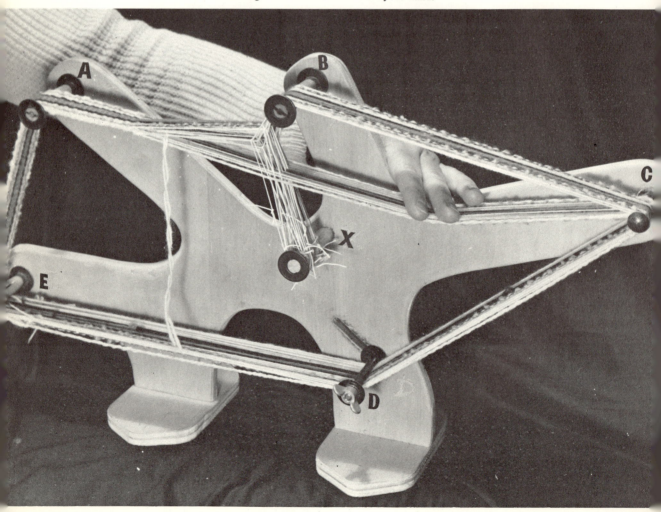

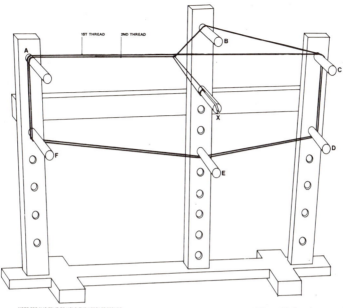

NOTE PEG X IS SPLIT TO HOLD THE HEDDLES SECURE

Fig. 10 b An upright Scottish inkle loom

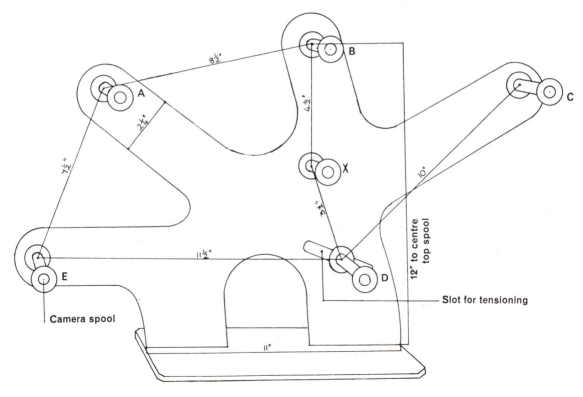

Fig. 10 c A home-made inkle loom. Height of loom may be increased by extending length of legs and changing tension to vertical slot.

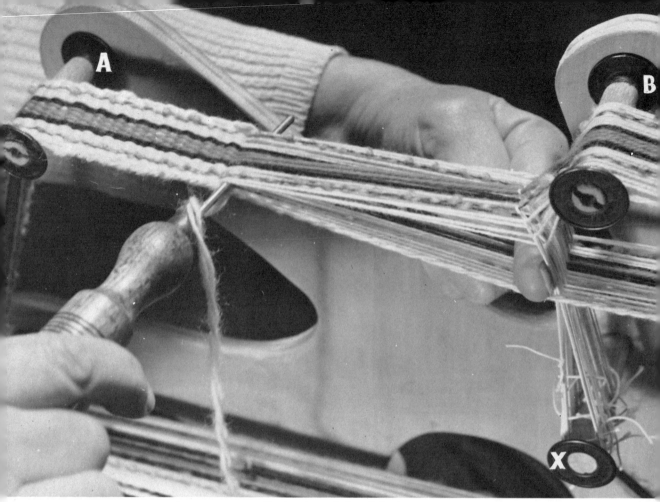

Beating the weft threads back.

A few suggestions for weaves on these looms are – cords for bags, coloured linen or cotton braids to add individuality to a frock, a matching belt and hair band, a wider strip for cuffs on a frock, a man's tie in either home-spun wool or machine-spun wool, bookmarkers in coloured weaves, and edgings of all kinds.

The character of the yarn used makes the texture and the design. It can take a thick warp with a thin weft, and this weft scarcely shows at all. Very tight beating of the weft will give a different effect from that obtained when the weft is beaten loosely. A wool tie in home-spun yarn needs to be beaten loosely so that when tied in a knot it is not too bulky.

As the warp threads show up more than the weft, colour needs to be placed in the warp. Always tie any new threads at peg A on to the previous thread, then no unsightly knots will spoil your weaving. The warp colours need to be balanced evenly, i.e., the centre strip should have the same number of colour changes on either side of it. It is advisable to make the weft colour the same as the outer edge of the warp, the reason being that it is easier to make a neat edge with the same colour.

A few suggestions for weaves

An attractive variation in warp stripes can be made by using a tie-dyed yarn balanced with a plain yarn as follows:

All inkle loom threading starts from the left, so read the drafts from left to right.

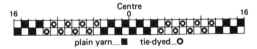

plain yarn.....■   tie-dyed.....O

Threading draft

Warp stripes can be broken from the straight line look by threading the different colours in an interlocking "toothed" draft. The following is a draft in 3 colours:

Finished appearance

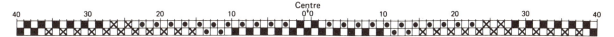

Threading draft

The above suggestions were in plain weaves, having the warp yarns of equal thickness, the only change occurring in the colours. Now thread the inkle loom with a coarse and a very fine thread so that all the coarse ends will be on the "open" shed and all the fine threads will pass through the heddles. Press down on the shed and you will notice that all the fine warp threads are raised. By inserting a thick weft thread the resulting weave becomes a raised textured weft fabric. Interesting pick-up techniques can be done on these coarse and fine warps as well as bold skip patterns in thick brightly-coloured yarns and embroidery stitches.

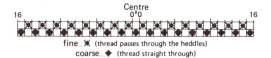

fine...✻ (thread passes through the heddles)
coarse....✦ (thread straight through)

In working pick-up patterns on the inkle loom make a shed and hold it open with the left hand, start the weft from the right-hand side, and with the right hand pick up the required warps from either the top threads or the lower threads, whichever form your pattern, and work across towards the left hand. Leno twist and Brooks Bouquet (see *Creative Crafts with Wool and Flax* p 44-45) are easy patterns to work and look very effective on this coarse and fine threading, particularly when they are worked on the fine threads only and the coarse ends form the background.

Maori Taaniko patterns are very interesting to do on the inkle loom and because the warp ends are held under tension the weaving is much quicker

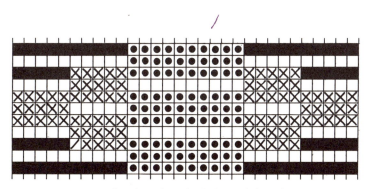

A pattern for skip threads. Coloured threads can be used double

to execute than in twining. One very effective pattern worked in blue and white on a white cotton warp is from S. Mead's *The Art of Taaniko Weaving*, page 71 No. 20 worked on 17 warps Turn the pattern sideways and weave the first row with blue yarn for 14 warps and 3 with white. 2nd row with white yarn for 2 warps and blue for 15. 3rd row with blue yarn for 2 warps, white for 12, blue for 2, white for 1, 4th row with blue yarn for 2 warps, white for 13, blue for 2, 5th row with blue for 4 warps, white for 11, blue for 2. 6th row with blue for 2 warps, white for 2, blue for 2, white for 6, blue for 5. Continue following the pattern sketched on the graph paper.

Thread the loom, weave several rows of weft, then weave in 3 or 4 matchsticks or toothpicks if the width is narrow—otherwise use a wider stick. This makes sure that the weft is weaving straight and also gives a firm area to beat against if hard beating is desired. Now work on a closed shed. With the weft thread on the left hand side pass it *under* all the warp ends, thread the required number of beads on the needle, pull the thread very taut, and the beads up in place between the warp threads. Hold them there with the first finger of the left hand while the needle is passed from the right side, *over* all the warp ends and *through* the holes in the line of beads. Notice that you have one weft thread under and one weft thread over each warp, and that the weft goes around each pair of outer warp ends. Any knots rejoining weft threads should lie inside the beading rather than joins at the outer ends.

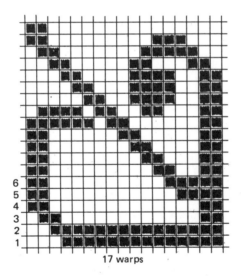

17 warps

RIGHT: A beautiful example of inkle loom weaving by Dorothy Mirth Young of New Hampshire, USA.

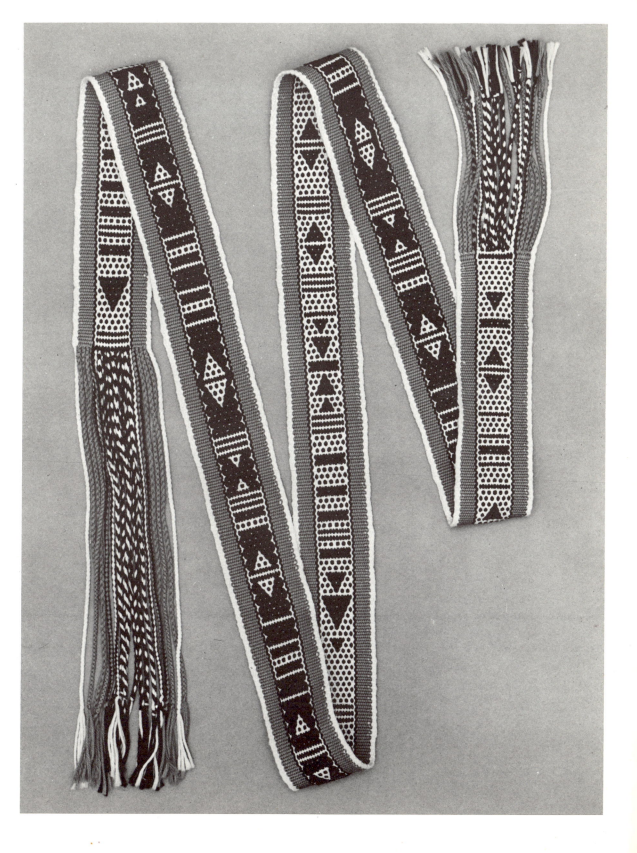

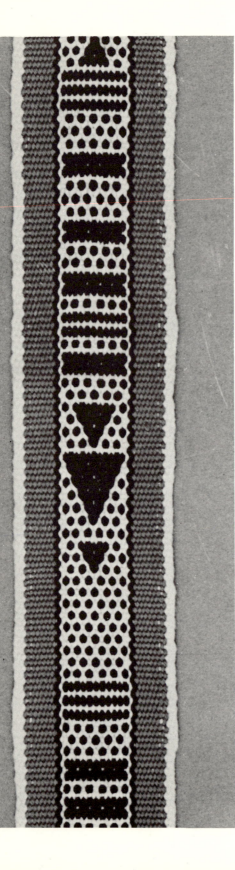

The warp ends are threaded in the following sequence:

Reading from the left. . 4 yellow threads

            14 green threads

            2 black threads

            36 for the centre patterned area threaded 2 yellow and 2 black

            2 black threads

            14 green threads

            4 yellow threads

The material used is a soft thick cotton and all threads are of uniform size. The weft is yellow, the same as the outer 4 warp ends.

The finishing fringe is a 4-strand rounded braid worked as follows:

  Take A over B and C to the right

  Twist C over B to the left (these are the outer ones on left)

  (the order is now C,B,A,D.)

  Take D over A and B to the left.

  Twist B over A to the right (these are the outer ones on right)

  (the order is now C,D,A,B.)

  Take C over D and A to the right

  Twist A over D to the left

  (the order is now A,D,C,B.)

  Take B over C and D to the left

  Twist D over C to the right

  (the order is now A,B,C,D.)

LEFT: A closer view demonstrating the weaving technique. The pattern is of American Indian origin.

A shaft-loom and its parts (see fig. 11)

The type of 2-shaft loom selected for illustration is a table model with two heddle-frames. The same principles of construction and manipulation apply to a 4-shaft and to a pedal loom, but a greater variety of weaves are possible on the 4-shaft. The width of the 2-shaft can range from

8–30 in., the smaller width being ideal for weaving experimental samples before mounting a long warp on a large foot-loom. Colour combinations can be worked out on a small warp before buying or making the quantity of thread necessary for a large piece of weaving.

Apart from the increased width and length, the more advanced features in the 2-shaft in comparison with the inkle loom involve the heddles being more firmly supported on heddle frames or shafts, which are raised and lowered by means of a lever. This changes the shed through which the weft passes much quicker than changing it by hand. Also a beater with its reed is incorporated in the construction to cater for the increased number of threads. Rollers, too, are added to carry a longer length of warp.

A 2-shaft loom showing the method of raising the heddle frames with the lever on top

Note the following features:

a. Two heddle frames made of strips of wood (a top and a bottom for each frame) are spaced to hold the cotton heddles in position. The top shaft of each frame is attached by means of tapes or cords to the harness roller at the top of the loom. This roller holds the lever. To be sure of making a good wide shed attach the bottom shafts to a harness roller also. These shafts are removable and must be about $\frac{1}{4}$–$\frac{1}{2}$ in. shorter than the space between the centre posts to allow them to be raised and lowered easily. By pulling the lever forward or backward the heddle frames may be raised or lowered as needed. Tapes are strong calico, $\frac{1}{2}$–$\frac{3}{4}$ in. wide. Cords made from $\frac{1}{8}$ in. blind-cord or loom-cord can be set in a groove to prevent slipping, or tied to screw eyes set in the shafts.

b. Both the warp and the fabric beams are locked in place with a ratchet.

c. The beater pivots on two upright side legs from the lower side-beams of the loom frame. These legs can be either on the inside or the outside of the frame. Whichever position is chosen, make provision for the beater to be adjustable so that it can swing from two or more grooves. This allows a wider beating area and saves shifting the warp too frequently.

d. The top of the beater lifts off so that reeds of different sizes may be inserted when desired. The purpose of the reed is to keep the warp threads evenly spaced. The teeth of the reed are set at certain spacing to the inch.

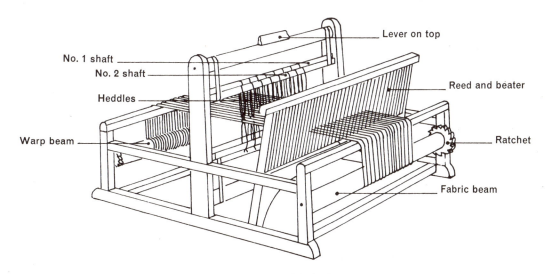

Fig. 11. A 2-shaft loom with the lever on top.

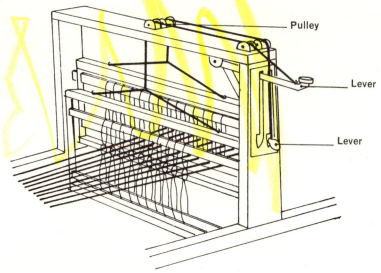

Fig. 12.   A 2-shaft loom with levers at the side.

For an all-purpose reed choose a 12-dent; its width will depend on the width of your loom. Reeds can be purchased in standard sizes or made to order.

e. Apron-rods (once made of cloth and hence the name) can still be made of cloth but are more usually thin flat pieces of smooth wood tied at an even distance from the warp and fabric beams. They are used for tying on the warp threads in small bundles and to hold an even tension across the width of the warp.

A 2-shaft loom showing method of raising and lowering the heddle frames with levers placed at the side

Notice how the cord is attached to the top of the heddle frame and runs over the pulley at the middle of the frame to connect with the hand levers. The lever locks in position, and when released will automatically fall back into its original position. The heddle shafts can swing loosely or slide up and down in grooves cut in the inside edge of the two upright pillars (fig. 12).

Heddles and how to tie your own (fig. 13)

A heddle is a threading device made of either thin lightweight metal or of string. It is an advantage to know how to make a string heddle in case you need to add more to your shafts at any time. Take care to tie the eye through which the warp ends will be threaded to the exact level of your other heddles. The eye opening is usually $\frac{3}{4}$ in.

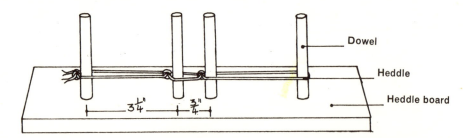

Fig. 13.   Method of tying heddles. Measurements for 8-inch heddle given. Total length may be increased by adding to either end of heddle.

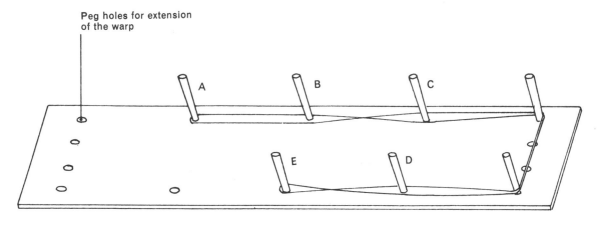

Fig. 14.   The first thread on the warping board.

wide. Make a heddle board with four dowels or four 6-in. nails, the standard spacing is as follows:

For a 6" heddle ..	2"	$2\frac{1}{4}$"	$\frac{3}{4}$"	$2\frac{5}{8}$"	2"
For a 8" ,, ..	2"	$3\frac{1}{4}$"	$\frac{3}{4}$"	$3\frac{5}{8}$"	2"
For a 9" ,, ..	2"	$3\frac{3}{4}$"	$\frac{3}{4}$"	$4\frac{1}{8}$"	2"
For a 10" ,, ..	2"	$4\frac{1}{4}$"	$\frac{3}{4}$"	$4\frac{5}{8}$"	2"
For a 12" ,, ..	2"	$5\frac{1}{4}$"	$\frac{3}{4}$"	$5\frac{5}{8}$"	2"

Estimating the amount of yarn needed for the warp

This depends on three factors:

a. The number of warp ends per inch, 12 ends in a 12-dent reed if you thread one warp end through each dent in 1 inch. Sometimes you may require finer texture and will thread two warp ends to every dent, and your number for calculation will then be 24.

b. The width of the warp, to which you add approximately 3 per cent for shrinkage and selvedge. Thus to a finished width of say 28 in. add another 2 in. = 30 in. Now we can have some idea of how many warp threads to wind on the warping board – 30 in × 12 in. or, for the finer texture, 30 in. × 24 in.

c. The length of the warp: In addition add an extra yard. This extra allows not only for shrinkage and contraction in weaving and finishings, but also for wastage in tying-up and the unwoven end of the warp.

We can now assess the amount of yarn for the warp. For a woven length of warp of 10 yards (a finished length of 9 yards) and a woven width of

Showing threads on the warping board.

30 in. (a finished width of 28 in.) with 12 ends per inch, the amount of yarn is 30 in. $\times$ 12 $\times$ 10 = 3,600 yards. For the finer cloth it will be 30 in $\times$ 24 $\times$ 10 = 7,200 yards. The weft generally takes a little less yardage than the warp. Make a practice of weighing every warp and recording it before mounting it on the loom.

Winding a short warp

The threads made on a warping board will lie on the loom in exactly the same order as they will be threaded into the heddles and reed. Figure 14 shows a warping board set for a length of 2 yards. By adding more pegs at the two ends, a warp of up to 7 yards can be made. Always test the length with a piece of string measured to the warp length you require.

Two crosses are made on the warping board – one between B and C, and one between E and D. Tie the first thread at A and guide it over B, and under C, round X and Y, over D and under E. This makes one warp end. The return trip makes the second warp end. Continue around E and under D, back round X and Y, over C, under B, to A again. Repeat this cycle until the required number of ends are on the warping board.

Securing the crosses

While the warp is secure on the board three ties are essential (fig. 15):

a. Tie the cross between D and E. The loop over E is the end that goes on the warp beam.
b. The loop at A is the beginning of the warp. Tie threads here to mark where to cut ready to thread them through the heddles and reed.
c. Tie the cross between B and C. This one

shows the order of the threads for entering into the heddles.

Using a warping mill

Warps of more than 7 yards are made more quickly on a warping mill which revolves on a base. The uprights on the mill are spaced 1 yard across, and the lower bar holding pegs D and E are adjustable. The crosses are made in the same position as described for the short warp, i.e., between B and C, and between D and E (fig. 16).

For further speed it is usual to warp with several spools placed on a spool rack, the end threads of the spools being threaded through a paddle (fig. 17).

Tie yarns to first upper peg on warping mill at A. To make the first cross, hold the paddle in the right hand; with the forefinger of the left hand hook the back threads on paddle to the front, passing over the first front thread, pick up the first back thread, over the second front, pick up the second back, over the third front, pick up the third back, etc. Thus the group of threads forming the first cross are all on your left forefinger. Slip the left thumb up between those threads and the paddle. The cross lies between your forefinger and thumb. Slip this group of crosses onto pegs B and C.

Now the left hand is free to rotate the warping mill round and round clockwise. When you reach pegs D and E wind the group of threads under D, over E, round E, back over D. This forms the D and E crosses.

Change the paddle to the left hand, rotate the warping mill anticlockwise with the right hand, grouping the bundle of threads directly over the previous line of threads. Make the crosses between B and C in the same manner but reversing the

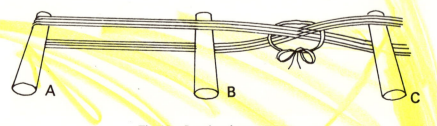

Fig. 15. Securing the crosses.

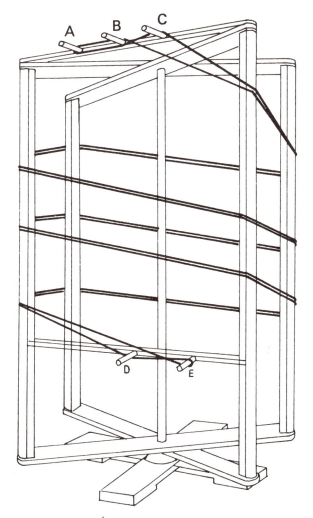

Fig. 16.   A warping mill (drawing taken from Dryad Equipment Catalogue).

on the mill. Secure the crosses with string ties as shown in previous diagrams.

Chaining the warp

Starting at the bottom of the warp board or mill (i.e., at pegs D and E) release the bundle of threads, grip them firmly in the left hand, wind the entire warp round and round the closed fist of the left hand in an over-and-under motion. Tuck in the looped end from peg A and slide out the left fist.

Alternatively, instead of winding around the left fist, make a series of small chains, i.e., make a loop and pull part way through this a few inches of warp, repeat this every 12 in. or so.

Threading and "dressing" the loom (fig. 18)

Take the apron-rod from the back warp-beam and slide it through the loop of threads made at peg E. Tie the two ends of the string which secured the D and E cross to the ends of this apron-rod.

The warp threads must now be spaced on a raddle. If your warp was designed for 12 threads per inch place groups of 6 threads in each raddle space. Have the middle of the raddle clearly marked and place the middle of your warp there. Tie the raddle securely at both ends immediately the warp is spaced on it.

Now transfer all (the warp, the apron-rod, the

position of the hands, i.e., with paddle in left hand and using forefinger of right hand, pick up the back threads, slip right thumb up near the paddle, and transfer the cross from your fingers to pegs B and C.

Pass the paddle with the group of threads around peg A, turn the paddle down and under so that the threads are anticlockwise and change the paddle to the right hand. Make the cross at pegs B and C as described above and continue warping until the required number of threads is

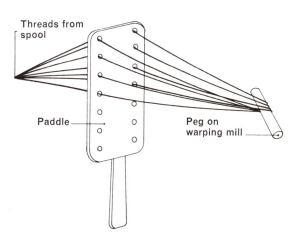

Fig. 17.   The use of the paddle.

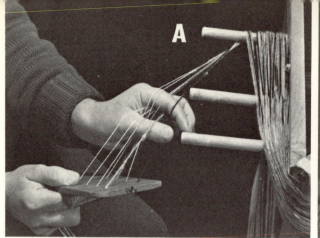

Making the first cross.

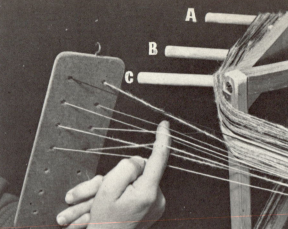

Changing paddle to left hand.

securely-tied raddle) to the loom. Tie the apron-rod back in position on the warp-beam. Clamp the raddle on the loom or rest it on long poles placed on the loom for this purpose. Take the other end of the warp very firmly in both hands, pull tightly and shake the warp. This is where a helper is invaluable because the warp must be rolled on with firm and even tension. Remove the stop-pin from the ratchet, place strong brown paper or several sheets of newspaper around the warp-beam, and wind on the warp.

The shed sticks are now placed in position and tied securely (fig. 19). Release the string originally used to secure the cross at B and C. On no account must the order of the threads in the cross be lost or altered. The warp threads come over and under the shed sticks in the correct order for threading and can be moved in pairs along the shed sticks. Cut the warp threads at A where the string was tied. Using a threading hook or fine crochet hook and, beginning at the right-hand side, enter the warp ends alternately through the eye of the first heddle on the No. 1 heddle shaft; and then the first heddle on the No. 2 heddle shaft. This is for tabby only. (See fig. 24.)

Loosely tie the ends in groups of four to avoid slipping back. Place the reed in the beater. Starting again from the right side, untie the first bundle of four threads, enter each one into the dents of the reed in exact order. A skipped dent will leave an open space in your weaving.

As before, tie small bundles of threads together in loose knots as you go along the reed. Release the ratchet of the fabric-beam and allow the apron-rod to pass over the front of the loom and tie the warp ends in bundles on this apron-rod, making the tension even.

Remove the shed sticks – re-check the tension on the warp. Weaving can now begin.

The insertion of the weft consists of three operations:

a. Making the shed;
b. Passing the shuttle through;
c. Beating the weft threads in place.

Even weaving follows when these movements become rhythmical.

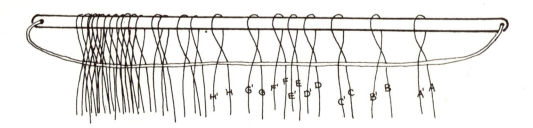

Fig. 18.   The end threads securely on the apron-rods.

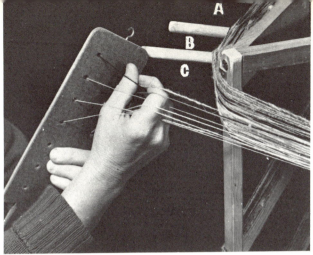

Slipping right thumb up to paddle.

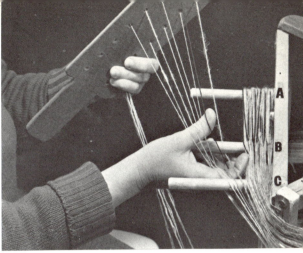

Transferring the cross to pegs B and C.

A few practical facts for consideration:

A new shuttle is started by overlapping two ends for about $\frac{1}{2}$ in. in the same shed.

Very thick yarn should be mitred.

If weaving narrow stripes the weft can be carried up the side selvedge edge.

For even weaving make sure the beater is at right-angles to the warp threads, otherwise the finished work will be crooked.

Most looms cater for about 5 in. of weaving before shifting the warp, but the beater can be moved forwards or backwards on its grooves.

The strength of the beating depends on what type of weaving you are doing – a wool rug requires firm, heavy beating; tapestry weaving has the warp beaten out to make the weft predominate; soft material needs very little hand-pressure on the beater because the swing of the beater is sufficient.

Always pass the shuttle from the right when the front shaft is down – thus the position of the shuttle will indicate which shed comes next.

Pin a tape measure along the selvedge edge to check the measurement of your weaving.

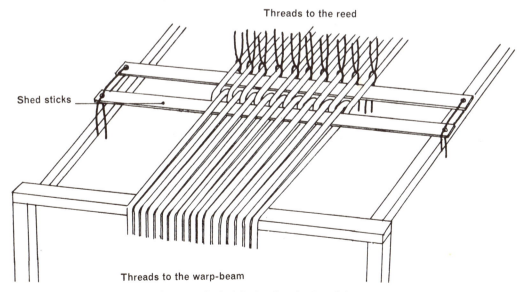

Threads to the reed

Shed sticks

Threads to the warp-beam

Fig. 19. Shed sticks holding the B and C cross.

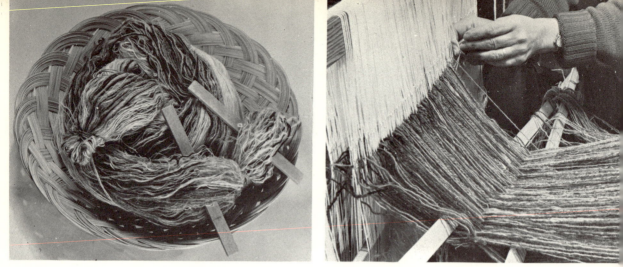

Left: A chained warp with shed sticks placed between B and C cross.
Right: These shed sticks remain in position while threading.

Rug weaving

Very interesting and effective floor rugs can be made on 2-shaft looms using the same weaving techniques as already described. The looms can be either horizontal or upright, but must be very strong to take the heavy beating. The upright takes less space in a room, and most rug looms have two pedals only. Another advantage of the upright model is that when several colours are being used simultaneously as is done in tapestry-weaving, the small bundles of colours can hang downwards out of the way, whereas in a horizontal warp these need to be continually shifted to avoid tangling – like the twisting of threads in Fair Isle hand-knitting.

It is possible to make a rug in sections on a rug frame-loom made from a large picture-frame. This can be mounted on legs if necessary. The proportions for the rugs are better rectangular rather than square: for example, 2 ft 6 in. × 4 ft,

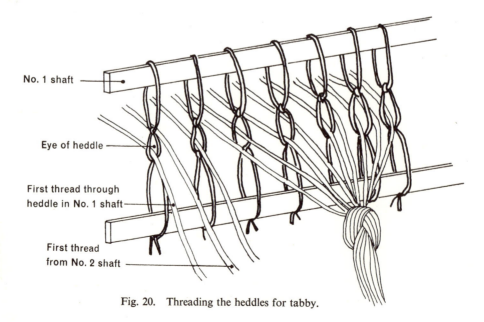

No. 1 shaft

Eye of heddle

First thread through heddle in No. 1 shaft

First thread from No. 2 shaft

Fig. 20.   Threading the heddles for tabby.

3 ft × 5 ft, 4 ft × 7 ft. The design of tapestry-woven rugs should be plotted on graph paper first but tufted rugs, being simpler in design, can be sketched with less detail. See fig. 21.

For the warp use a strong 8/4 cotton or 2-ply flax twine and/or carpet wool and about 6 ends per inch—this will depend on the size of the frame on which you are experimenting. A notched rod at both ends will help to keep the warp threads straight, and two wooden clamps at top and bottom will hold the warp taut.

Make a shed by lifting each alternate string with a shed-stick and then turning the stick on its side. The reverse shed is made by leashes tied in groups of six and the weaver pulls them forward by hand.

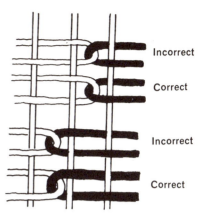

Fig. 22. Stepping to keep a flat surface and to avoid slits.

There are three types of rugs to try out on this rug frame.

a. The tapestry or Khilim rug. This is a reversible rug. The weave is plain tabby with the weft beaten down to cover the warp entirely – all the design is in the weft.

   Put the weft through in loose loops in a bow effect, comb it in place with your fingers first, then finally push it firmly in with a strong comb or a kitchen fork. Beat it firmly with a strong shearer's or other metal comb. (This applies to the picture-frame when you haven't a proper beater.) The purpose of looping the weft is to prevent the selvedge sides from pulling in.

   Thick homespun wool makes an interesting texture for these rugs. The patterns made by breaking the line of weft into small colour areas of dark and light contrasts must be looped to avoid slits, which are permissible in tapestry pictures but not in floor rugs. Figure 22 shows the correct and the incorrect way of doing this. The rule is: link so that each loop passes over its fellow if it passed over its last warp end, and under its fellow if it passed under its last warp end. By looping correctly the joins are less bulky. If slits do occur, hand-sew them afterwards.

b. The tufted or Rya rug derives its name from the village of Rya in Sweden, but knotted rugs are not exclusive to this area, a similar tuft or pile effect having been developed for many

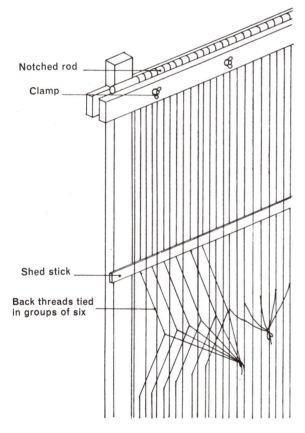

Notched rod

Clamp

Shed stick

Back threads tied in groups of six

Fig. 21. Section of a tapestry-rug frame-loom.

Texture of 2-ply homespun wool tightly beaten in a tapestry rug.

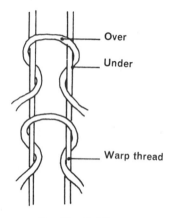

Fig. 23.   Tufting.

c. Finger-twisted fleece wool rugs. Because so much fleece wool is available in Australia and New Zealand this method of rugmaking has become exceedingly popular. Second-grade wool can be used – scour it well, tease and card it into long rolags. Twist these rolags a little as

years in Asia Minor, Caucasia, Persia, and other countries. All these rugs have a shaggy look and because of this need a simple design with delightfully blended colours.

There are several ways of knotting. Figure 23 shows a standard method which certainly is an ideal way to use odd ends of wool imaginatively. Knots are tied on each pair of warp strings across the loom – on the flat warp without any shed. A strand of wool that is going to make the loops is put over the two threads, one end passed to the left and taken under the left warp thread, brought back to the middle, looped over the right-hand warp thread, then under it, bringing it back to the middle again. The two ends are pulled tight to make the knot. Weave several rows of tabby before tying on the next row of knots. Beat firmly to keep the knots in place.

Tufting is not confined to Rya rugs – it is used as decoration for edgings, bags, cushion covers, curtains, etc.

Texture of unspun, finger-twisted wool rug.

you place them in the shed. If beaten very hard they will keep in place without tabby weave in between, though sometimes the tabby adds to the design. Fine rolags make a different texture to thick ones. Whatever the size make sure the beating is so firm that the rolags cannot be shifted with your fingers, otherwise your rug will not wear well. For preference use a white warp for a white rug. Very attractive colour combinations can be woven with vegetable-dyed fleece wool all blending with natural grey and brown fleeces.

Try, also, in your rugmaking a combination of finger-twisting and Rya, using the Rya knots to accent the design; the finger-twisting gives a textured background.

Finish your rugs either with fringes knotted in single or double rows of reef-knots, or thick chain-stitch; or bind with soft leather concealing the reef knots holding the warp ends.

Bibliography

Atwater, Mary Meigs. *Byways in Handweaving* (Macmillan Company, New York).

Brown, Hariette J. *Handweaving for Pleasure and Profit* (Faber and Faber).

Cherry, Eve. *Handweaving* (English University Press).

Davenport, Elsie. *Your Hand-Spinning; Your Hand-Dyeing; Your Hand-Weaving* (Sylvan Press).

Grierson, Ronald. *Woven Rugs* (Dryad Press).

Lloyd, Joyce. *Dyes from Plants* (published by the author).

Mead, S. M. *The Art of Taaniko Weaving* (A. H. & A. W. Reed).

Spinning Wheels, published by the Ulster Museum, Ireland.

Worst, Edward P. *Foot-Power Loom Weaving* (Bruce Publishing Co. USA.).

Marion L. Channing *The Magic of Spinning* (privately published, USA.).

Other Reed Craftbooks include:

Creative Crafts in Wool and Flax by Molly Duncan

A natural sequel to this book by the same author. Planning threads, knitting with homespun wool, weaving with wool yarns, flax and its threads, colour, and embroidery in flax and wool.

Dollmaking by Gwynne Nicol

An illustrated description of the whole process of designing and dressing dolls with a valuable chapter on marketing ones dolls to the best advantage.

Dyes From Plants by Joyce Lloyd

Equipment, supplies, methods, dye stuffs, tie-and-dye are all described, together with dyes from native plants of Australia and New Zealand. Chemical dyes are also discussed.

Pottery for Pleasure by Elizabeth Lissaman

A unique feature of this book is its guidance on New Zealand and Australian clays and raw materials. Clay preparation, pottery with and without a wheel, decoration, colouring, glazing and firing. A splendid book for beginners.

Index